A ROSE
IN A DARK PLACE

POEMS FROM THE SOUL

TAMEKA RIDLEY

Dedication

This book is written in honor of my ancestors, my children, and generations after me. May we heal from all the secrets burdening our lives and rewrite our history.

CONTENTS

Disclaimer

You know what I love about poetry
The deepness
The realness
And the swag
So I write poems from
Deep within my soul

With every word I write,
I get to really show the world that I'm motherfucking dope
Fuck all the shit
Anyone has ever said about me
My life is a gift

And
My story
Had to been written
The vitality of my message
Will live on
Through my words...
There is strength in my spirit.
Poetry makes me
Feel
Indefinitely Dope

Like a Goddess...

The power of my thoughts
Mixed in with the fire

Tameka Ridley

In my voice
Leaves hearts racing
And young minds wondering

Who is this woman?
I am what God made me to be
More than a woman
More than my past
My name is Tameka Ridley
And believe it or not
This is my story.

Planting The Seed

I remember my Auntie's wedding like it was yesterday.
I was probably five or six years old at the time
The most magical part I remember about her wedding was
that
I was a flower girl
That meant I could get dressed up
In a pretty dress like Cinderella
I wore satin white gloves
With my name ring on top so everyone could see
Yes I was flossin'
Stuntin' on 'em with my cute lace socks with the bows
And my white patent leather shoes with a heel
My hair in Shirley Temples curls
The same way my mom liked to style hers
We met up with family where my grandma lived
When our ride pulled up it was the
First time I saw a limousine in front of Webster Projects
We went inside dressed in fancy clothes and excitement
And I didn't really know what was next...
When we arrived at the church,
Everyone smiled when they saw me and took my pictures.
When I heard the music,
I knew it was time to walk in.
Someone put their hand on my back
And the ceremony began
I saw everyone looking at me and my lil' cousin
As we walked down the aisle
With our flower baskets and
I let the rose petals fall from my hands
My lil' cousin didn't understand what we were supposed to do

Tameka Ridley

So, she started picking all of the petals up and putting them
back in her basket
And our family laughed
I felt so much love
Then all eyes were on the Bride
She looked stunning coming down the aisle in a long white
gown
With my grandpa on her arm
Her wedding planted a seed in my heart
And I began to dream about the day I would get married.

Baby Girl

One thing money could never buy is

The love a daughter has for her father

Her love is priceless and pure

Her admiration for him is endless

Daddy is big and strong

He is the protector and provider

Of all her hopes and dreams

And she dedicates her future to him

Every move she makes

Is for his praise

And joy

Her love is unconditional

Tameka Ridley

My Surprise Birthday Party

I was 9 years old when I had my first surprise birthday party.
It was one of the most memorable days of my life because it is
the only birthday party I remember having, with both my
mom and dad as a kid. It was extra special because my
friends and family were there also, and I had a pinata. For the
rest of my life, I will hold on to the joy I had at my surprise
birthday party.

A memory I will always hold on to
Like a dream, I hope to live every day
SURPRISE!!!
My heart drops
Then skips a beat
Like a rollercoaster ride of Happiness

Wrapped in all my innocence
Love of Family
From what I could remember
Playing with my cousins
Having fun celebrating
Hugging & laughing with my grandma

Opening gifts and birthday cards from grandpa with money
inside
That's what I thought birthdays would always be like...

The Day I Became A Fatherless Child

I came home from school one day
And my daddy wasn't home
The house looked the same but different
Suddenly a strange feeling came over me
Sadness

But before it fully settled in
I ran to check my diary
And I noticed my last entry was ripped out
He had to have read what I wrote
Which means he knew what mommy did

She cheated but so did he
I just never thought my dad would leave
The sin of their infidelities broke me and
In that moment, I knew he invaded my privacy
Yet I felt like I betrayed him

I used to tell myself that's probably why he didn't take me
with him
That day he stole the last page of my diary

And never came back home again

Heartbroken, alone
And only 9 years old
I was forced to grow up
Without
A father

Family Secrets

We kept secrets from the rest of the world
Treating me like daddy's big girl
I walked to school by myself since kindergarten
And warmed up frozen dinners all by myself

Do you remember when you took me to "the spot"
And left me outside by a payphone?
You made sure before you went inside
To show me how to get home alone
You know "Just in case"

Thank God you always made it back to me
Then we would go home together
and you would go into your bedroom
locking the door behind you.

I can still smell the marijuana
The smoke made us cough a lot
Me and my little brother
Learned to get used to it
Like how we got used to feeling unprotected

I still can't believe you never looked backed when you walked
away
Maybe I was the problem.

I couldn't look happy enough for you to stay
Or it had something to do with the time you hit her

8

A Rose In A Dark Place

In front of me and I called the cops on you

Sometimes I wish I would've just told the cops the truth
Snitch on daddy because he hit my mommy
And when I tried to intervene... and save my mommy
he hit me too
I remember at 9 years old hitting my own father with a
broom
That beating still hurts me

I cried in a warm bath with alcohol
soothing my welts and pain
then I slept through the night like a baby

Pretending

Right after my dad left,
I begged my mommy with tears
To pretty please not send me to the babysitter

I even promised to be good
But mommy had to work
And pay bills all by herself

Just too afraid to tell her
Because at a young age I knew very well
That there were repercussions of being a snitch

So, although I didn't want to go, I went
And while Mommy was at work
I laid down while my babysitter hurt me

After a while,
I learned to take the pain
Pretending to hold my breath underwater

She made me promise not to tell my mother.
And 25 years later,
I still kept my promise.

Sin

I tried to find myself in the church
My ex-best friend went to
They preached
But
All I heard was
"God made Adam and Eve
Not Adam and STEVE!!!"

Conflicts arose in my body
The sins of my flesh
Lived in my everyday thoughts
Hating myself
For my attractions to women
And disgusted with the ugly pimples on my face

Could someone just love me for me?
I wanted to feel loved
And accepted
The way I used to.
But I don't know if God could ever forgive me for what I let
happen to me

My 1st

My homegirl from the block
Introduced me to her cousin
He was my 1st
A lil' cutie with a tongue ring
And he had his eyes for me

I liked that he flirted
And was hitting my spots
I started watching a few pornos
But wasn't sure if
I was ready or not

His kisses were juicy
Sucking my lips
He used one hand to grab my hips
And his other hand felt me get wet in between my thighs
Then he picked me up in arms

And I lost it to him
On his aunt's kitchen counter
The moment lasted but a whole minute
At first, I thought it made me walk different
But it didn't, and I was over him.

Curved him
And then he copped me a ring
I didn't marry
That clown
I was only 16

All Men Are Dogs

I bet you think that was fucked up huh
That I slept with him
Then dumped him
This virgin was far from clingy
So what?! I didn't care about him
And he lied when he said he cared about me
He wasn't nothing but a creep
That liked to cheat

He was supposed to be my man
But he was on the "down-low"
How could he take my virginity and then propose
Knowing all along he liked to sleep with men
But I'm not surprised
My mom taught me from young
All men are dogs.

A Rose Is Still A Rose

I needed someone to...
Love me
Make me believe in myself
To tell me I was beautiful, smart
And should educate myself
I needed someone to mentor me about the struggle of being
brown
And being a woman
I needed someone to teach me how to defend myself
So, I don't get fucked up in the hood
Or end up dead
I needed someone to help me
Provide me with opportunities
So, I can live instead of going out every day fighting to
survive
All I ever wanted was to live and be free

But when my father left
Things went left
I decided to find my way
In the streets
Fronting like I was tough
Until I believed that shit
Street niggas told me I was fly
They defined my intelligence
And my worth
And when they got tight
They called me a bitch

A Rose In A Dark Place

But after a while
I wasn't having that shit
Didn't have a friend that believed me
There was no one to tell my babysitter
To stop touching me
I had to learn the hard way
Running the streets
At 11 years old
With fake friends who
sliced me and left a buck 50 on my face

Unforgiveness

Since I was 9 years old
Every single day of my life
I've felt the agony and loneliness
Of not being daddy's little girl anymore
Missing my father's love
Patience
Attention
And wisdom

Never understood
Why he was gone,
Didn't call
and didn't try
Never understanding why my children could never get to
know him
He'll never be a grandpa like mine
Cuz he missed all of their birthdays

I dream about his funeral all the time
How would I feel?
What could I say?
Would I even go?
Would I even know?
From what I know
I would say my father was intelligent
A street smart scholar who
Made time in between his drug addiction to teach me
Most importantly book smarts

A Rose In A Dark Place

And the street codes that kept me alive
And helped me survive
The meanest streets of the Bronx

I learned tough love
Cause his absence made me feel invisible
My father is the reason why love hurts me so much
The void in my heart
He left
Damn near took my life
And the cycle of unresolved issues continues...

Because I still love him
Yet my memories will never forgive him
For what his neglect put me through

Travis

My little brother became a man
In the absence of our daddy

We got calls from private numbers
From daddy
So, we couldn't call him back

He called to tell us he was a preacher
He must've needed God to forgive him
For leaving
Travis
I'm glad you don't remember
But I do

And since I do...
I can't forgive him
For robbing us of the love and life we deserved.

Instead, we were left
With memories we want to forget.
Stripped of the protection we needed

You leaned on me
When you got beaten
And eventually

I left you too

A Rose In A Dark Place

I'm sorry from the bottom of my soul
I wasn't strong enough to carry the burden
Of protecting you
From the Bum
My mother loved

So, I blame our father
"The preacher man"
Who probably was
Reading the Bible
To his other kids

While I tried to take the beatings for you
I was just a kid myself and didn't know what to do

How could he have
Abandoned us
And created a new family
And really think that God forgave him

I had to tell you
Daddy wasn't coming to pick us up
Every time he stood us up

Sometimes we'd argue
Because you wouldn't give up
We cried and cried
And I acted out

Full of anger

And what did Dad do?
Pray?
Was that the best he could do?

Tameka Ridley

His wife never liked me.
I can never forget her screaming at dad hysterically,
"You love her more than me!!!"
He responded, "No I don't!"
Right in front of me.
It broke my heart.
When I look into his eyes now
I see his deceit and I feel nothing inside me
He's just a preacher man that can go to Hell
Without my brother and me.

Mixed Feelings

These
Indescribable
Emotions
Leave me in a
Speechless
Rage
With
A Plate full of mixed feelings
And a side of regrets
Love
That's hard to swallow
I'm full from
The resentment
I'll bag up my hurt
To go

Tameka Ridley

Shut The Fuck Up!

You don't understand me
Don't try to

Always looking at me with those big tearful brown eyes
That annoy my every existence

I just can't fucking stand the way you stand there like you
care!
Smothering me like chicken I couldn't even feed a dog!

Nagging me to handle your responsibilities!!!
Until I can't stand to hear your voice

Drowning out your waste of suggestions for my life
Increasing the volume of chaos in my mindset

I just can't fathom why your mouth is still moving
When will you just shut the fuck up!!!

Your ignorance is naive to how much I despise you
You keep wishing on a star you'll never touch

Maybe if I just close my eyes
And sit still in the darkness
You will finally disappear

Black

My mind won't let me lie down
My mental is locked up in a jail cell
With so many demons inside
I am Hell

Please tell my mother that her angel has no wings to fly back
home before dark

No more visions of colors
All I see is BLACK!

Black men who can't breathe
Black women who don't know their daddies

All I see is BLACK!

Black children who don't want to learn in school
So, they learn life in the streets

All I see is BLACK!

Black boys who can't buy Skittles from the store wearing a
black hoodie
Black girls who can't see their natural beauty

All I see is BLACK!

Tameka Ridley

Snitches getting stitches
Feens on their knees
Carrying keys in their bellies

So high they don't have sexualities anymore
Because they have to sell their bodies for a fix

Looking in the mirror at this unrecognizable person
Defeated by drugs and poverty
All I see is BLACK.

CAN I LIVE?

Broken Promises...
Every time my tears fall
My eyes hate you more
And the more my heart despises you
The more my mind spirals
Into a twisted obsession
Of every moment I've ever shared with you
My soul declares war!
On your spirit
My eyes have seen violence
And my heart has felt so much pain
Leading to my tears
And fears
Of losing myself
In the midst of this storm
Reality is
Because of my skin
I'm lost in this struggle
With Love
For those who hate my hair
And others
Who whisper my skin is dirty
I'm grappling
To exist in this world
And growing impatient fighting for the freedom
To love my skin
My melanin descended from my ancestors
Deserted in America
with no investments
Just life choices and no security

Tameka Ridley

The Cycle Of Feeling Unloved

I guess I'm gonna have to talk myself out of being upset
again...
Unresolved issues
For my entire existence

I wanted people to respect me
For who I am,
And have become

But my own insecurities
Kept attacking my feelings like,
Why doesn't the world love me?

Until I learn to love me
And not the things of the world,
I will never be respected as a Queen

Forget

I will never forget those trash ass men that
Referred to this Black Queen as a Bitch

They invaded my palace
To steal my treasures from me
And got away with it

I will never forgive them and the motherfuckers who knew
Cuz I will always remember how you didn't care

My ferocious aggression
Towards you every second
Will poison your conscience
And devour you whole

You
Worthless
Miserable
Fuck Boys!

Tameka Ridley

These Streets Will Eat You Up!

These streets ain't playing with you!
They will chew you up and eat you out

Robbing you of your dignity and integrity
Don't be another statistic
Becoming heartless to survive

I survived the streets
And I'm here to tell you
The streets don't make you
Don't let them break you!

Bars From High School

It's that bitch
What up?
You ain't fucking with me
Cuz I'm realest bitch in the NYC

You know nothing about
Ride
Or
D-I-E

You know nothing about style
And getting money
You never popped mo
Smoked dro

Never ever had a doe
I'm never ever scared bro
We can go
Toe to toe

Let's get poppin' bitch
It's whatever's clever
Yo you mad at me
Cuz you never get no money hoe

No Respect

She ain't got no respect for herself
Rocking a "God is Dope" shirt
But she is far from a Saint
Everything that comes out her mouth is ratchet

She gets off on being rude
And disrespectful
Gossiping and talking shit on social media

She judges the world like she is God
And doesn't have any love
She hates herself
So she tries to form weapons against you

She's a
Straight up
Hater
Who talks mad shit
Because she ain't shit herself

She tries to dress nice
But expensive clothes
Will never make her beautiful on the inside

She wastes all her time and energy
Hating on you

When she should use that same energy
To get a damn life
Point Blank Period.

A Fight That Changed My Life

I remember being in high school
First or second period
And my two homegirls

Talked me out of leaving my classroom
While we was walking down the hallway
And they tell me
Some bitch wants to fight me
They said she been looking for me all morning
Unbothered
I grab my knife
Tucked away inside my Northface coat
I ain't never seen her fight
I knew she was soft
I fought at school all the time
Then suddenly, the bell rang like
My name did in the streets
Tameka will fuck up anybody!

So my homegirls walked with me to my next class
You know "Just in case"
A little agitated, I walked ahead of them

Starting to get hype at the thought of my gangsta being tested
again
I look around and see shorty
Standing on my left, across from the police

Tameka Ridley

I'm like okay
This bitch don't really want beef
She stepped to me talking trash and I shut her down to walk
away
And shorty sucker punches me from the back
Now it's too late for talking
I gotta hurry up and beat her ass
Then dodge the police to make it to my next class
She hit me so hard
I thought blood was falling out my eyes
Still throwing my hands with shorty
I saw my boyfriend in all red chilling in the cut
When I looked into his face
I knew I had to fuck her up
In absolute rage
I blank out and couldn't stop beating her up

She tried to run
I yanked her hair
And slammed on the ground
Dragged her down the hall by hair
And punched her in the face over and over again

The police yanked me off her
And pushed me to the floor
They searched me and found the knife in my coat
I got suspended

And sent to an Outreach center
I met people I want to forget
That fight changed my life
And I ended up transferring to a new school.

You Don't Want It With Me

Back in the days
You couldn't even step to me
I promise you
The old me
Would've never let you finish your sentence
Before I'd chin check that jaw
I'd drag your little ass up
And down the street

But I can't take myself there
My subconscious tells me
Because you're not worth it
You feening to see the old me
And in one instance I could lose everything

Lose all my freedom
Sitting behind bars
In an orange jumpsuit
And cornrows
Cuz I cracked you in the face
Bashed in your brain
And kicked out your two front teeth
With my Timberland boots

Maybe I pulled out a shank

And pressed it hard against your throat
Just to hear you beg the old me
Not to fold you.

Street Life

If you really want to make 'em mad
Keep doing you

Make your money
Stay fresh
And get an education

There is a career
A husband, a house and a car waiting for you
In your future

Brush the haters off
Let 'em talk their shit
Cuz that's all they gon' ever be
The shit they talk

And if you really get 'em tight
They gon' wanna fight
And know that
You might not get a fair one

There are some fights that you can't avoid
Especially when you from the streets

But pick and choose your battles wisely.
Like I always say, "It's better to walk away,
So that you can live another day."

Discernment

I have become a harsh judge of character
I expect friends to be loyal
And therefore, have none
My enemies will always remember my name
My raft is a force
Even I am afraid of

Unleashing my pain through art
So that I may live in a world

Without Bars

Without
The Handcuffs
Of oppression

I expect my lovers
To always
Want to fuck me

Love me
And/Or
Hate me

Know that
The world will
Remember me

Tameka Ridley

Sorry I'm Not Sorry

I'm sorry
That no matter how much
Love you give me
I can't feel it
No matter how many times
You say I love you
I don't hear you
I have no words to reply
Remaining silent but not speechless
Hoping we'd vanish from
Whatever this is...
You call this a relationship?
Truth is
You're a joke
This "relationship"
Ain't nothing but a thang
And so, I remain silent
Staring at a Nothing
Feeling empty
I could never love you
Your heart knows
You live a lie
Because of you
I'm Heartless

Boy Bye!

Deuces
Your ugly, jealous ass didn't appreciate me
And didn't respect me
At all

Your trifling, lying ass
Had the nerve
To come into my bed
With more lies,
bitches and no money

You thought you were the shit... huh?!?!
And had the audacity to put your hands on me
While I carried our child
There was nothing left to do
But get fed up as women do
And change the locks
Like mama used to.

Powerless

My greatest regret in life
Would be not saving my baby
Only to God will I ever fully disclose my heartache
Large mountains of palpitations in my body
Desperate for air, I grab my chest
Dropping to my knees
The rapid rush of pressure
Makes it hard to breathe
I look up towards the blurry skies
Surrendering my revengeful spirit to the pit of my womb
Bleeding out
Rivers of buried veins
Wounds that will kill me
Unless I heal

Coming To

Acknowledgment
In order to heal
I must accept the things that I cannot change

It's difficult
Because I want to fix everything
And save everyone
While carrying the weight
Of the world
And a book bag filled with huge obstacles
The size of the universe

The thoughts in my head are complex combinations of
Never-ending questions filled with doubt
I deflect
By fighting the voices in my head
Discouraging me & oppressing me
Making me feel helpless

I have to fight the thoughts in my head
Because the reality is, I cannot change everything
But that doesn't mean things won't still change

It may take time
Or more people
And joint efforts

I have to fight negativity

Tameka Ridley

Because my peace is worth fighting for
And for the things that I can change
I accept the honor and responsibility of making a difference
In my community
Making the first step
To find meaning in my life.

Surrender

Cry on your knees
Lay your heart
On the floor
In front of me
Give me
Your soul
So, I can save you
Close your eyes child
Trust me

Tearful

My dad was my Tupac
He made me hardcore so I could survive in the streets
He was slim, tall and brown skin
Handsome, black and intelligent
He looked so strong with no shirt on doing
Pull-ups
On the monkey bars
I remember him always rocking a fresh pair
Of Clark Wallabees on his feet

He took me to the official Kangol store
I never saw so many hats and Original Gangsters
He took me shopping and said get whatever you want
Feeling spoiled from a drop of his attention
I saw him every couple of years
And never told him how I feel
If only he knew back then
All I ever wanted was
Some attention and to spend time with him
I wanted him to wipe away my tears
Erase the pain away
And heal my wounds
I guess I needed too much
Because that day never came

He use to be my everything
He was the first man to ever break my heart
Since then, I have never fully healed

A Rose In A Dark Place

Because the life I knew and loved
Wasn't the same
He made me feel special when I was delicate
Then left me to grow up feeling abandoned and lost
like a rose in a dark place.

Mother

You have always made brown
Look amazing
Your natural glow
Inspired me to grow old

Your long dark hair
And smooth, glistening skin
Made me respect you
Mother

Your essence lives
In my genes and traits
Mother Legacy
You stayed with me

Kept me grounded
And great things came
And there's more to come
Thank you

Shrimp & Grits

A mother's love
Is strong and wise
Intense at times
But it tastes like
Bacon on a Sunday morning
With scrambled eggs on the side

Her love chills the mimosas
And her smile fills you up
Like a bowl of shrimp
And cheese grits
She blesses your life and generations after

Tameka Ridley

To My Other Mother

Dear Mrs. Collins,

We miss you every day.
Your sweet energy
Tastes like a cold cup of Cherry Kool-Aid
With extra sugar.
Your smile was the light in the sky
I comfort your Sun with love for you.
Burning like a flame on a candle.
Your presence is still here.
Praying God could bring you back to us
Because your presence blessed us tenfold.
Love, the lover of your Sun
Mother, you are cherished
By us all
Your spirit... defines poetry.

It Was A Wednesday

I knew he was my soulmate
Way before we made it official on Facebook
Asking me to be in his life forever
With a Topaz ring

Forever means forever
Diamonds are a dream
Not meant to be
My love is true

Craving his time and affection
Obsessed with his eyes
Mesmerized by his kiss
Feeling paradise in his arms

He is an escape into the bright sunset
Barefoot in the hot sand
Sensual smiles
And wedding wishes

Surprises I will remember for eternity
My father walked me down the aisle to our song
"This is why I love you"
He gave me to my Prince Charming

We exchanged our rings
Under soft white lights arched over the two of us

Tameka Ridley

We kissed in the finest of fabrics blessed before our family

And then we held hands
And walked over the broom
Our marriage was the best birthday gift ever.

The Urge

He's Big, Tall and Handsome
His eyes tell me he's ready
I want to lick his face whole,
Taste his tears
And fuck away his fears

He's so fine
So glad he's mine
I want him every minute
All the time
I want him to make my lotus flower drip

He makes me crazy
With his kiss
The Good Lord knows
Homeboy got some juicy lips
I want to make him moan

He knows just what to do
To get me in the mood
I want him now
But I'mma chill out till he makes a move
Every time we make love it feels like our honeymoon

Passion

My thoughts be all over the place
Like my hair after wild sex
And forgetting to put my bonnet on
Man we be getting it on

Pleasing me with his gifts
Loving me with his lips
Trusting me with his heart
Missing him when we're apart

Longing for his presence
Every chance I get
I can't focus on anything but him
About how I want to fuck him again

Exotic poses
Slipping off my robe and climbing on top of him
Desiring his thrust
And looking into his eyes
He gives me every inch of his body
I feel his soul
And lose control
But I still have a grip
On his throat
Before I kiss him

Wanting some passion
I can feel in my toes

A Rose In A Dark Place

Makes me cry when I moan
Makes me beg for some more

Becoming obsessed with his touch
And hypnotized by his Love
When he's inside me

Feel Me

Ask me anything you want about love
It's so ironic that I would sit here
Reflecting on my newfound Peace and Joy
Blessings that I'm unworthy of
But receive thousands of

I'm sitting here reflecting on my blessings
Of unconditional love

We give to each other
And make sacrifices for one another

We ain't Papoose and Remy
But in our hood
We hold hands down the street and
When people see us
They see
Black Love

When they see us
They recognize and respect
We got Real Love like Mary J.
They see
A Mother and a Father
A Queen and her King

They see a deeper love than no one could ever know

A Rose In A Dark Place

Ask me anything you want about love
While I reminisce and share my memories
Today is the fifth anniversary of the day
I met the love of my life
Isn't it iconic?

There are secrets to our Super love
A bond we will always share
My heart still celebrates the day that we met
And I looked into your eyes
I am one word
BLESSED

With Love that reflects itself
Like a reflection in a pond
Looking at me
Looking at you
Looking at us

And when you touch the water
Your reflection remains until you walk away
And we don't walk away
Our love isn't a reflection in glass
Because we don't break

But in water our magic happens
And we never disappear
We float. No, we fly
Like Aladdin and Jasmine did on the carpet
We ride for each other like Bonnie and Clyde

I'm his Wife and Boo
His Lover and Moon

Tameka Ridley

He's my King,
My Tribe,
My Bae,
My Life.

I love my husband
Truly and deeply
Fully and completely
And that's why...

I love that you asked me about Love
And as I sit here reflecting...
Love is also about making sacrifices like sharing my life
I just hope that you feel me.

From Me To You

You gave me a foundation
With your commitment
And reconstructed my life
You improved me
And we became a family
You became a father
To my children
And make us happy
You are my husband
And I truly love you
With all my heart
You taught me the meaning of loyalty
Friendship and true love
By being there for me whenever I need
You are everything to me
This poem is forever
Like my love is for you.

Kya & Sheila

My daughters are my angels
I worship the ground they walk on
Adoring their beauty and uniqueness
Looking at them
I see my reflection

They are the best of me
My heart, my soul, my everything
Their joy and happiness
Is my motivation to be an inspiration
They are my purpose

A diamond in the sky
And blind faith
Are the meanings of their real names
With love and time
I hope to inspire them to be great
Both special in their own way

Melting my heart with their smiles & laughs
I wish I could be with them forever
Let my spirit live on in their hearts
Shine bright princess like the North Star
This poem is for you.

Love always,
Mommy

My Biggest Fear Is That I Will Hear My Daughter Say...

Mommy I want
To be a model
That pops bottles with rappers
Maybe even have a baby with Bow Wow

For Xmas
Can I perm my hair, get some fake eyelashes,
and a lace front?
Oh and some new Jordans
And some poppin' Mac lip gloss
Please!
All the girls in school
Tease me and call me ugly
In front of all the boys
And everyone laughs

When I grow up
I'mma show all of them
I'mma get plastic surgery so I can look just like Cardi B
I'mma get me some big titties
A flat stomach
And a fat ass
I'mma have a coke bottle shape
And every nigga in the universe gonna want to marry me

They gonna buy me

Tameka Ridley

Louis Vuitton bags
And diamond rings
Just because... I'm beautiful

I'mma live in a mansion
And guess what
I'm never gonna have to ask you for shit
Anymore

Merry Xmas

If Only Life Worked That Way

What if choosing a life for myself
Is like I'm shopping for new shoes
'Can you help me?'
I'm looking for a new life

'What's the occasion?'
Getting tired of my old one, so I'm looking for a new one.
'Sure, I can help you with that.'
'But first tell me, what kind of life are you looking for?'

I'm looking for a life
That's comfortable
And comes with extra support
But that really fits my style

'Well, you're in the right place. I'd be happy to help you.
Tell me a little bit more about your style.'
It's unique, bold and colorful
Sexy, fun and feminine

'I have the perfect life for you
Just wait right here.'
New shoes...
If only choosing life for yourself was that easy.

Woke

Lost in an unimaginable world
In a tornado of grief
Undiagnosed with psychosis
Just crazy hurt
Open your eyes
You're not qualified to judge me
You simply choose not to exercise the power to save me
I am left praying for me
To feel whole again
To be hugged
And feel real Love
Instead, I continue to suffer from
Abandonment and
Blind Abuse
From a system of pain
Endured by my ancestors
Mentally enslaving generations of children
Who feed off the breast of single mothers
In the projects
Meant to keep us down
Imprisoned by prejudice
Lack of resources & opportunities
Suffocated by
Racism
And drive by tragedies
Gang signs
Fathers buried by oppression
On the back of their necks

A Rose In A Dark Place

Spirits that scream "I can't breathe"
Our bodies lie face down
With our hands behind our back
In handcuffs to die mercilessly
Without peace
And without justice

I Am A Queen

I remember the first time I was recognized as a Queen
I was in my 30's
At the African Street Festival in Brooklyn Navy Yard
I wore a beautiful African dress
Full of bright orange colors and kente cloth designs
My jumbo box braids were up in a high bun

I was searching for more Afrocentric clothes to add to my
collection
And a handsome black man tried to get my attention
"Hey Queen"; he went
Selling copies of his book

Him being an author made him more admirable
But I belonged to a good man
And when I thought about my boo
My conscious gloated from ear to ear
I wanted to sit back and enjoy all his love
Respect and admiration
Couldn't let temptation take a hold of me

Instead of losing myself in the moment, I accepted his
acknowledgement
and embraced the handsome young king with class
Giving him my eyes full of attention

Once he started talking
I was sold

A Rose In A Dark Place

By his realness
And purchased his book

As a Queen
I showed him love
And bought his book
For my King
To celebrate our anniversary

I carry myself like a Queen
Yet I am still a Rose
Whether or not a handsome man notices
My intellect, loyalty
And love
Is a True gift

Tameka Ridley

Show Me Love

I want to show everyone I love them
While I'm still here
But I just don't know how

I've lost so many people
And I've only shown my love
With tears no one sees

It's a cycle
Of not knowing
How to love

All I feel is pain
And heartache
The saga continues

Until the day,
The spirit of an angel finally touched me.
I felt safe.
Then, I began to
Pray.

Letter to My Grandmother

Dear Grandma,

I'm sorry. I'm sorry for so many things I've done in life, but what really eats away at my heart is that I wasn't there for you when you got sick. How I loved you, but I didn't show you because I was too busy hiding my bruises from you. I didn't want you to see me in a dark place.

Your last words comforted me with your love and forgiveness. You said, "I love you," and I said, "I love you too." And then you said, "I hope to see the baby soon." I wondered how you knew. Deep down, I said, "me too." Two weeks later, we finally got to see you. But it was at your funeral, and all I could do was cry.

I miss you grandma, and I wish you were here. If only you could see me now, you'd have been so proud of me. I finally got my life in order the way God intended for me. I have a husband, two lovely children, and an associate's degree. I'm going to keep on striving for the moon. When I reflect back on my life, I know I'm alive today because of you. When I was young, you had me get down on my knees and prayed beside me. And you also told me the hell off when I needed you to. Thank you, Grandma, I love you.

Until we meet again,
Tameka Ridley

I Love You Grandpa

I don't remember my grandfather ever saying "I love you"
But he showed me with his actions
He was always present
Grandpa was the one man I could always count on
Now he's sick from cancer
Bed bound with broken femurs
And I feel helpless
Because I can't heal him
I know that I have made him proud
Showing him love with my tears
And with my prayers
I feel his pain every day
I know he just wants to rest
But I can't help but want to save him
I want to scream
"Live"
For me
PLEASE
But instead I show him with my tears
That I will love him always

Don't Worry About Me!

When you hold me in your arms at night
My tears feel like they will never stop falling

The closer you get
The farther away I push you

You hold tighter
Trying to rock me to sleep
And you fall sound asleep from the exhaustion
While I lay awake for hours
Drowning in my own sorrows

I escape silently
Leaving you in bed alone
Wouldn't want my cries to wake you

And so I run away
Locking myself away
Into even deeper sadness

Feels like I'm falling fast
Just haven't hit rock bottom yet
Then, I begin to feel sorry for my kids.

I wipe my face

But even with the door closed,
They hear my cries.

Tameka Ridley

Too afraid to open the door
And let anyone see my tears
I sit up pondering new ways
To hide my pain.

Tired

I tried to show you
I love you
By not arguing
By suppressing my negative feelings
And lying beside you

I tried to show you I love you
When I told you
Spend the night out
But the truth is
I wanted you to stay

But another part of me
Wanted you to go

My mind wants to tell me
That anything you enjoy that's not with me
Is cheating
Yeah that sounds crazy out loud
But it's the truth

Loving you makes me crazy
I tried to show you that I love you
By being faithful
And suppressing the urges to step out
On our marriage for a nut

Tameka Ridley

I tried to show you I love you
By taking care of us
I tried to show you I love you
Time and time again
But I still feel empty

I'm tired
Of being tired
Of being sad.

I need an inspiration
To help me elevate
My spirit.

Your eyes look at me with sadness
That's why I keep my head down
Looking at the lines of these hardwood floors

I can't stand to look into your soul
Without tearing up
I just want to hide my pain
From you
So, you can just keep enjoying your day

Born Guilty

There's a voice in my head
That won't leave
It's taunting me
"Tell me. Don't show me."
Haunting me in my sleep
My anxiety from those words
Won't let my eyes stay closed
Everyday my thoughts run around my fears
And insecurities
Protecting me from opening up myself

I'll show you
How I feel
Through a picture
But telling you
Is like snitching on myself
And being black in America
I've learned not to persecute myself
I have the right to remain silent
But at what cost

My spirit
My craft
My freedom to live
In silence, I hear those voices become louder
Consuming my Brain
Poisoning my mental
Into Anguish and pain

Tameka Ridley

Like thousands of fresh lashes on my back

34 years a slave
To the discrimination of my skin
And gender
"I can't breathe"
"You're suffocating me"

Torturing my hope
Attacking my faith
My fight to reach my goals and aspirations
Are my protest

All I ever wanted to be
Was free
But I can't because I'm trapped in this brown skin
34 Years a slave
To oppression in America
I've been coerced into
Embracing the black struggle

"Go back to Africa!!!"
Wait, what?!?!
I didn't choose to be Black
My skin chose me
Only to be pushed into
A never-ending
Fight to survive
Racism in America

Another voice says
"Suppress the pain"
I listened to that voice

A Rose In A Dark Place

So, I can move forward everyday
But inside
My heart feels
Like
A dead black man
Handcuffed on the concrete

Everyone's watching
And recording from their phones
A voice screaming for mommy

Being black in America
Feels like screaming
"I can't breathe"
To a cop who doesn't care

Being black in these streets
Is like being in a jungle
"The streets don't love nobody"
Yet we learn life in the streets
Witnessing
Drugs, Guns, and Violence
Fooling only ourselves
That we have power
With Materialism

Giving money to corporations
That benefit from our
Mental slavery
Imprisoning our spirits
Into poverty
We have so much in common
With the criminals we see on TV

Tameka Ridley

We're the same color
And the world has taken away our liberties

We are all born guilty
In a country built on
White supremacy
Being Black in America today
Is the definition of
Injustice.

Something

Say something deep
Something that touches my mind, body, and soul
Make it real
Make it feel authentic
Let your words comfort those in need
Let your heart fill with empathy, love, and understanding
Just show that you really care
For others
For our community
Our Nation
Our People
Say something
Please
Because just standing there
Doing nothing
It's not only an injustice
It's plain disrespectful
It's a fucking abomination

Assume the position and
Say something to unite us
Not divide us
Say something
Before you get canceled
Like businesses during the George Floyd protests

I will not be anyone's nigga

Tameka Ridley

Nor will I be your enabler
Nor will I be killed in vain
At the hands of violence and systemic racism
Before you speak when you look at me
See that
My brown skin
Doesn't make me inferior to anyone
My skin does not make me a criminal
It makes me beautiful
My brown skin is not a threat
Nor is it a weapon
Why can't you see that my brown is beautiful?
SPEAK!
Or lay down and stay down.

In Living Color

Thorns

Stamped on her body
Like your color
Pain
Following you everywhere you go
Oppressing you
Lowering your self-esteem

But not your worth
You are not that label
Your color
Is beautiful

It's embedded in who you are
Because without color
You'd be just a blank page
In no one's imagination
Visions

I woke up one morning
While it was dark out
And tried to remember your face in my dream

My mind goes a little crazy
But I control my thoughts with my pen
Or vice versa

Tameka Ridley

Maybe I just use my pen to convert my dreams of you
To whatever's socially acceptable
My pen controls the universe, rewriting history with every
word

You

Brighter than the stars at night
Your elevation illuminates God's Light
Beneath your curves of melanin blessings
A priceless masterpiece far beyond impressive
Your beauty is more than the color of your skin
Through your anointing, I find peace within...

A Rose In A Dark Place

Blinded by darkness
Her flower is plucked
Again, and again
Till the rose had no petals left
Her rose possesses beauty
In that dark place
Right underneath the razor-sharp thorns
Feel for it
The pain
Leaving unseen red trails in every direction
Not even
The rain could wash the remnants of blood stains away
Celestial rays of stars radiated over her thorns
For the world to see
Like fireworks in Crotona Park on Juneteenth
A little light shined on that rose,
and she never felt more beautiful.

Acknowledgement

Thank you for reading my book and congratulations for being inspired. May my life empower you to share your story with the world. Then boom! We honor our ancestors.

I want to give honor to God for making me who I am today.

I want to thank my family:

My Mother, Sheila Lawrence, for being my best friend.

My Father, Anthony Cassaberry, for teaching me street smarts.

My Brother, Trevor Cassaberry, for always keeping it 100 with me.

My Aunties, Debra Smith, Mercedes Joy Bullock and Vivian Cassaberry-Furby for mentoring me and encouraging me to further my education.

My Grandma, Johnnie Mae Cassaberry, for teaching me how to get down on my knees and pray.

My Grandpa, Herman Lawrence, for teaching me consistency.

Tameka Ridley

My Husband, Reggie Ridley, for understanding me, loving me unconditionally and being supportive of my accomplishments.

My Daughters, Kya and Sheila, for being the greatest inspirations in my life.

Also, I want to thank everyone at Hostos Community College for opening my eyes to a world of opportunities. Special thanks to Mayi Libfeld, Jason Libfeld, Carol Huie, Craig Bernardini, Sandy Figueroa, Amy Ramson, Ausberto Torres, Kelsey Hillebrand, Felix Sanchez and Linda Ridley for teaching me how to become a motivational leader. You never stopped believing in me and I am beyond humbled.

I want to thank my mentor, Neal Schick, for getting me in touch with Yael R. Rosenstock, founder of Kaleidoscope Vibrations, and Author Yolanda Sealey- Ruiz. I appreciate all of you for sharing your knowledge and words of encouragement.

Without all of your love and support, my book would not exist. I am an author, thanks to you. From the bottom of my heart, I wish you all peace, blessings and love.